I0103548

John Renwick Seager

The Law of Elections

John Renwick Seager

The Law of Elections

ISBN/EAN: 9783337253462

Printed in Europe, USA, Canada, Australia, Japan

Cover: Foto ©Suzi / pixelio.de

More available books at **www.hansebooks.com**

THE LAW OF ELECTIONS,

AS VIEWED IN THE LIGHT OF

The Election Petitions of 1892.

BY

J. RENWICK SEAGER,

AUTHOR OF

"NOTES ON REGISTRATION," "THE FRANCHISE ACT, 1884," "THE MUNICIPAL
ELECTION ACT, 1885," ETC., ETC.

London:

PUBLISHED BY HAYMAN, CHRISTY & LILLY, LTD.,

113, FARRINGDON ROAD, E.C.

1893.

ELECTION PETITIONS, 1892.

EAST CLARE COUNTY.

CIRENCESTER.

CENTRAL FINSBURY.

HEXHAM.

EAST MANCHESTER.

NORTH MEATH.

SOUTH MEATH.

MONTGOMERY BOROUGHS.

ROCHESTER.

STEPNEY.

WALSALL.

WORCESTER.

CHAPTERS.

		PAGE
I.	Associations	9
II.	Treating	20
III.	Marks of Distinction	25
IV.	Undue Influence	34
V.	Agency	41
VI.	Election Expenses	44
VII.	Practice	46
VIII.	Employment of Voters	49
IX.	Voting in Two Divisions	51
X.	Disputed Ballot Papers	53
XI.	Relief	59
XII.	Costs	62

PREFACE.

The General Election, 1892, has produced its batch
of Election Petitions, and the public has had once
more opportunities of seeing how unscrupulous
agents, and misguided, over-zealous friends may
endanger a candidate's election. While, on the
one hand, a beneficent providence, in the form
of an Election Court, may save him from the
effects of those illegal acts by stretching the powers
of relief given them by the Corrupt and Illegal
Practices Act to the fullest extent, a Court dif-
ferently constituted may unseat him for some
trivial breach of the same Act, or, owing to a
difference of opinion between the judges, may
retain him in the seat, although, so far as the
public are able to judge, evidence has been given
of an extensive breach of the law.

The puzzles of the Corrupt Practices Act have not
received much elucidation by the decisions of the
Election Courts, and, in spite of Mr. Justice Vaughan
Williams' remark, that he "did not believe that
in these Acts, fairly construed and applied, there
was any trap or pitfall into which a candidate,

determined to conduct his election honestly, need
fall," the questions upon which light is needed,
such as, " When does an election begin ?" are still
as dark as ever, and some conclusions have been
arrived at contrary to the spirit of the Act, and not
at all in favour of that freedom of election or limitation of expense at which the Act was aimed.
In the following pages an attempt has been made
to place before candidates and agents, and members of the public interested in elections, a state-
ment of the law as laid down by the Election
Courts in 1892 upon the questions submitted to
them. The reports quoted from are those of the
Times, which appear to be the fullest and most
accurate.

Some of the results of the inquiries are so un-
satisfactory, that either the Act has been improperly
interpreted, or it will be necessary to have fresh
legislation on the subject, of a more stringent
character, capable of putting down with a strong
hand the disgraceful conduct which has, in some of
the cases, been exhibited by the agents of the
candidate or by his supporters.

SUFFOLK HOUSE, E.C.,
February, 1893.

THE LAW OF ELECTIONS.

CHAPTER I.

POLITICAL ASSOCIATIONS.

ONE of the most difficult questions which has exercised the minds of Candidates and Agents is as to the position of an Association with regard to agency. Previous decisions on the subject are somewhat conflicting. The question has, however, been discussed in the recent cases of the Hexham, Worcester, Rochester, and Stepney Petitions.

At Hexham, an entertainment had been organised by the Conservative Association; railway tickets to the place of entertainment were supplied at less than cost price; while refreshments were provided at a less sum than the contractor could supply them for, the deficiency being made up by the candidate's agent, who was secretary of the association.

Mr. Justice Cave, in giving judgment, said: "The corrupt practices which were charged against the respondent sprang mainly out of the acts of certain of the respondent's agents, and of the divisional and local Conservative Associations and branches of the Primrose League. There was nothing to be said in the abstract against associations for the promotion of either Conservative or Liberal views so long as they resorted solely to things which were likely to produce an effect upon the reason of those to whom they addressed themselves. But it was otherwise when they endeavoured to acquire popularity for political principles by giving them treats and entertainments. If, in endeavouring thus to promote the election of a Unionist, their actions were recognised by the candidate, that would, of course, be quite sufficient to make the association—at all events, the executive committee of the association—his agents, and the candidate would be responsible as long as he chose to acquiesce in their endeavour to support him and to procure his election. Up to May, 1891, there was no fault to find with the Conservative Association, but, in the report then issued, district associations were recommended to hold entertainments at suitable seasons. That was a dangerous thing. There was always temptation, in case of loss, for people to subscribe to pay the deficiency, and that involved treating, which could not be too strongly deprecated. . . . As to the Chesters entertainment, on August 15th, the railway fares were given at reduced prices, and tea was provided at less than the contractor could supply it for, and the result was that there was a deficiency of £35. The entertainment was attended by a great number of people, and was calculated to increase the popularity of Mr. Clayton (the respondent) among the larger number of voters who had no great political interest one way or the other. The total of the sums expended by Baty (the agent) in this way came to £102. Treating was a particular form of corruption which could be practised with advantage at the present time, and a very small amount of treating was sufficient to procure a great deal of popularity."

Mr. Justice Williams, in the course of his judgment, also said: "The evidence had shown that the Hexham local association was not the only association which had a tendency to indulge in these pernicious picnics and entertainments, and he hoped that one result of this petition might be that the practices of these associations would be amended in the future."

In the Worcester case the Conservatives had formed what were called lodges of the National Conservative League, and it was said that these lodges held meetings at licensed houses at which every man who called himself a Conservative could have free entertainment.

Mr. Baron Pollock, in delivering judgment, said:

"There was one case of general treating, however, which he would have occasion to deal with, and that was the question of the Conservative Associations and other bodies who, by treating and other conduct, attempted to exercise an undue influence upon the minds of the electors. Modern times brought about modern manners, and the conduct of elections changed, partly owing to an alteration in the habits of men and partly by reforms enacted by Parliament; and at the present time, perhaps, the greatest influence used in Parliamentary elections was that of the political associations, and he, for one, would wish it to be distinctly understood that, if there were a political society whose establishment was permanent, and whose object was to watch the register, correct it, induce people to get their names entered upon it, and hold meetings and gatherings for that purpose, it was not to be too hastily assumed that because an election took place at some particular period, when every act done by the association might be in furtherance of the election, that the association or its members necessarily became agents for the candidate; and these acts, which would be done whether there was an election or not, did not necessarily become criminal because their effect might exceed their original object. It was not because an election took place that a political association should hold its hand and stop going on with its work in registration and other matters. But if the work of an association were directed towards the immediate benefit of a candidate, then he, for one, would look upon that political organisation with great suspicion. In the present case he did not think that such had been proved."

In the Rochester petition it was alleged that free smoking concerts were organised by a Conservative Club and a fête given by the Primrose League. At the first entertainment it was said that free drinks were given, and at the fête that the sum charged for entrance (3d.) could not possibly cover the cost of the refreshments supplied. Conversazioni were also organised by the Constitutional Association, which supported the Conservative candidate, and to whose funds the Conservative candidate had subscribed, in the course of the three years prior to the election, the sum of £900. There were a few other subscribers, but they were not very considerable.

Mr. Justice Cave, in delivering judgment, pointed out that with reference to the conversazioni, "it was obvious that the refreshment provided could not be supplied for the threepence charged, and he had come to the conclusion that those refreshments were supplied in that excessive quantity with a view to promote the election of

Mr. Davies, to influence the voters to give him their votes, and consequently that amounted to corrupt treating. Now, by whom was that carried out? All the arrangements were left in the hands of a committee of the Constitutional Association, of which Mr. Walter, afterwards election agent, was the secretary. The charge in the particulars was directed against Mr. Davies (the Conservative candidate) and Mr. Walter, and against them only. He very much regretted that it should be limited to those two persons, because it appeared to him that there were others who occupied a position of much greater responsibility than Mr. Walter, and who were really the guilty persons in this matter. He was unable to come to the conclusion that Mr. Davies knew of or assented to the provision of these refreshments at the time. With some degree of carelessness, he appeared to have left the whole matter in the hands of the executive of the Constitutional Association; and if a charge had been made in the particulars against any members of the committee, who it was shown had taken part in the supply of the refreshments, he should certainly have come to the conclusion that those persons were guilty of corrupt practices. He had not come to the conclusion that Mr. Davies did it himself, or that it was done with his knowledge or assent, but those who did it were undoubtedly agents of Mr.

Davies, and he must bear the consequences of their illegal acts. With regard to the Constitutional Association, it struck him as being an association which ought not to exist for the purpose of which this association existed. There was undoubtedly no harm in political associations, so long as they confined themselves to legitimate ends. The danger of them was that they were liable to be diverted towards illegitimate means, and undoubtedly it would be a wise plan, as soon as a candidate had been fixed upon, for these associations to suspend their operations until after the election was over, and entirely abstain as an association from taking any part in collecting any money, incurring any expense, or paying any accounts during the whole time the active candidature was going forward."

The lesson apparently to be drawn from these judgments is that a political association is entitled to carry on the legitimate work of political organisation and registration, and that a candidate may safely contribute to its funds for those purposes; but that it becomes a dangerous society if it steps outside those objects to endeavour to stimulate political interest by free or partially free picnics, concerts, or other entertainments, and that the candidate runs a great risk if he has either contributed money to the association or has accepted their support, and has adopted them as his agents under such circumstances.

In the Stepney case, two meetings were held under the auspices of the Conservative Association prior to the appointment of the election agent. At those meetings resolutions in support of the Conservative candidature were moved and carried. The expenses of the meetings were paid by the Association, and were not included in the election agent's return. Evidence was given that the funds of the Conservative Association were mainly supplied by the Conservative candidate, and that he was the president of the Association. The Court held that these meetings should have been included in the election return, but on application granted relief.

Mr. Justice Cave said: "As to the charge of payment of election expenses by others than the election agent, the expenses of the meetings of 9th and 13th June were not paid by the agent, and it has been established that that was an illegal practice, for it appears to me that they were part of the election expenses; they were, in fact, the commencement of the electoral campaign. They were paid for by two other persons, and the expenses were borne by Mr. Isaacson, and they ought to have been treated as part of the election expenses."

TRADE ASSOCIATIONS.

A very serious feature in the elections of 1892 was the organised electioneering by the Brewers' and Licensed Victuallers' Associations, and the decisions of the election judges must have caused consternation in the minds of all those who have desired that the spirit of the Corrupt Practices Act should be maintained. These associations expended large sums of money in holding meetings of those connected with the trade, in the distribution of literature and other matters, and in supporting by active work the candidature of Conservative candidates, on the ground that by so doing they were defending the interests of their trade. The money so expended was not included in any election agent's return, and therefore must have, in many instances, caused the amount expended in a candidate's interest to be in excess of the maximum allowed by the Act. The Courts, however, held that such expenditure was outside the scope of the Corrupt Practices Act.

In the Walsall petition, Mr. Baron Pollock, in delivering judgment, said "he thought the Licensed Victuallers' Association occupied a very different position from the Conservative Association, because it had a direct and vital interest in the contest on

the drink question, and he did not think their
action in holding meetings to promote their own
interests made them agents of the candidate."
While in the Stepney case Mr. Justice Cave said:
" As to the licensed victuallers' meeting, there is no
ground for saying that the expenses of it were part
of the election expenses. They were incurred by
them for their own purposes. No doubt they were
desirous to assist Mr. Isaacson, but it does not
follow that all the expenses they chose to incur
were election expenses of Mr. Isaacson. They may
have made themselves agents for him, so that any
corrupt practices of theirs might have unseated
him; but I cannot see that any expense they chose
to incur in promoting his election would be his
expenses of the election. If so, the position of a
candidate would be very deplorable indeed. He
would have no control over the persons who were
so acting for his benefit. I do not think, therefore,
that the expense of the meeting was part of the
expense of conducting his election; the expense
was incurred by the association for their own ends
and purposes, and was quite distinct from the
expense of Mr. Isaacson's election."

Whether the judges would hold similar opinions
if the United Kingdom Alliance had held meetings
in favour of the Liberal candidate is very doubtful.
It could hardly be said that they had any "vital

interest " in the contest from the drink-traffic point of view. The judges evidently considered the Licensed Victuallers' case from the trade or financial side, while the Temperance Party could only plead from a sentimental or moral aspect.

THE NATO... REFE... NCE ...'CI POLITICAL LIBRARY...

CHAPTER II

Entertainments organised by associations formed the subject of inquiry in the Hexham and Rochester cases. Evidence was given in the Hexham petition that a supper had taken place on November 21st, 1891, at Mickley, that the price of the ticket was eighteenpence, and that that payment included unlimited drink. Part of the food consumed was supplied free by local tradesmen; no political speeches were made, nor was the candidate present, but the gentleman who subsequently acted as election agent of the respondent attended and made a speech about football. The deficiency on the supper was made up by the same gentleman who was formally appointed election agent to the respondent on June 13th, 1892, but who, at the time of the Mickley supper, was secretary to the Primrose League and the Conservative Association. The Court held that the candidate had recognised the secretary of the Association as an agent by supplying the Association with funds through him, and that, in " the charge of making up the deficiency of the Mickley supper on November 21st, 1891, and in regard to the doings at the Seal on June 6th, 1892 (another entertainment), there were

instances of treating which were shown conclusively
to have been provided by Mr. Baty for the purpose
of inducing people to adopt or *confirm* themselves
in Conservative views at the election, which was on
June 6th known to be impending, and to vote for
Mr. Clayton. Both these occasions were occasions
of corrupt expenditure by Mr. Baty, and as, at that
time, Mr. Baty had been treated as Mr. Clayton's
agent, they voided the election."

In the Rochester case, where conversazioni were
held, and 3d. only charged for refreshments (see
p. 11), Mr. Justice Cave said : " It was obvious that
the refreshment provided could not be supplied for the
3d. charged, and he had come to the conclusion that
those refreshments were supplied in that excessive
quantity with a view to promote the election of Mr.
Davies, to influence the voters to give him their
votes, and consequently that amounted to corrupt
treating." The arrangements for the conversazioni
were in the hands of a committee of the Constitutional Association, the secretary of which afterwards
became the election agent of the respondent.

In the same judgment, Mr. Justice Cave dealt
with smoking concerts and birthnight clubs as
tending to foster among certain people an expec-
tation that, by joining these associations, they
would secure free meat and drink.

In the Worcester case, some evidence having

been given of treating by publicans, but denied by
the parties charged, the court seems to have treated
the matter very lightly. Mr. Baron Pollock, in
course of his judgment, remarked that "every one
who lived in a large town must be aware that publicans and every one else who went into the houses
sometimes did that which was not only bad for
themselves, but was a bad example, but which, if
done at the time of an election, might lead to suspicion, and perhaps actual proof, of malpractice in
influencing the minds of those to whom drink was
given. That something of the kind took place at
the time of the election there could be no manner
of doubt, but, at the same time, to say that it was
done with any ill intention, or that agency was
proved on the part of the people who had miscon-
ducted themselves, was entirely out of the question."

It is worthy of note that Baron Pollock was the
judge who so strongly upheld the right of publicans
to support their trade interests by organisation and
the expenditure of money outside the candidate's
election expenses.

Mr. Justice Wills, in the course of his judgment
in the same case, dealing with charges of treating
against a gentleman who was accustomed to treat
all round at fishing society meetings, held that "no
man was bound to abstain from hospitality because
an election was pending."

In the course of the Rochester inquiry, the judgments of the court at Hexham were referred to by counsel, who pointed out that before that judgment many lawyers as well as laymen had thought that such a transaction would have been outside the Corrupt Practices Act. Mr. Justice Cave, in answer, stated that the judgment must not be taken " as an intimation that any of the transactions there referred to standing alone would be held to amount to treating. In all cases you have to look at the whole of the circumstances, whether it is a repetition of a thing constantly done, or done merely once and never again followed up."

Baron Pollock held in the Montgomery case that an habitual drinker, who, when in his cups, treated nearly every one he came across, was not a proper person to act on a committee, but that his actions could not be considered corrupt. Mr. Justice Wills also pointed out that the practice of drinking and getting drunk could not be put a stop to at election times.

He dissented from Mr. Baron Pollock as to the effect of the treating by the habitual drinker, considering that " the reprehensible selection ought to recoil upon those who had been guilty of such culpable carelessness. In his opinion, this matter was sufficient to unseat the respondent." The judges, however, being divided in opinion, the petition was dismissed.

WE'RE BOUND TO WIN.

PLAY UP SWIFTS.

Vote for James.

Printed and Published by
W. Henry Robinson,
Walsall.

WALSALL HAT CARD.

CHAPTER III.

The 16th section of the Corrupt Practices Act of 1883 is very explicit with reference to the illegality of payment or contract for payment for bands of music, torches, flags, banners, cockades, ribbons, or other marks of distinction. The payment for bands of music, etc., is only prohibited when it is for the purpose of promoting or procuring the election of a candidate at any election. It is the *payment* or *contract for payment* which is prohibited. The service of a band rendered gratuitously may be accepted.

In the Hexham petition there were charges against the respondent that bands of music had been employed and paid for, and it was argued by counsel that the words of the section "at any election" were added to "candidate" to identify the person and not to limit the time. Mr. Justice Cave disagreed with counsel's interpretation of the section, and said "that bands of music before the election were not forbidden."

In the Rochester case, although evidence was given as to the purchase of flags and ribbons, the judges do not appear to have taken any notice of it in their decision.

In the Stepney case, evidence was given that the respondent, through his agent, paid for broad strips of canvas, upon which was painted "Isaacson for Stepney," these banners being suspended by ropes from houses on opposite sides of the street. It was contended by counsel for the respondent that these were not banners under the Act; that they were nothing more than canvas advertisements, and both counsel and the Court exercised their wits in a jocular direction as to the meaning of the word "banner." Mr. Justice Williams suggested that he did not think these were what the poet Gray meant when he wrote, "Confusion on thy banners wait," to which the petitioner's counsel retorted that when Shakespeare wrote, "Hang out our banners on the outward walls," they were just such banners as these. Mr. Justice Cave, in giving judgment, said, "Next as to the payment for banners. As to that, I am clearly of opinion that these 'canvas advertisements,' as they were called, are banners and nothing else. In order to get them made they went to a man who made banners, and they are described in the bills as 'banners.' If they were upon a stick at each end and carried, they would clearly be banners, and not the less so because not carried but hung out. It was suggested that the object of the enactment against banners was to preclude those kinds of marked distinction which might lead to fighting. I do not, however, think that such was the intention of the Act, for, if so, it would have made all colours and flags illegal; for whether paid for by the candidate or not, they would equally be provocative in character. It seems to me that the object of the Act was entirely different. It was to prevent the waste of money, and also to prevent men from getting a false show of power and influence by laying out money in bands and banners. There are a number of persons whose political opinions are weak, even, perhaps, to the extent of having none in particular, and who like to be in the majority, and everyone knows how important it is in elections to create an impression of success, as so many like to 'sail with the flowing tide.' It may be, therefore, that this, along with the prevention of waste of money, may have been the object of the Act in prohibiting banners, and it is obvious that these objects are irrespective of the way in which the banners are used, and whether they are carried or hung up. I think, therefore, that this was an illegal practice."

Mr. Justice Williams, in the same case, however, while agreeing with Mr. Justice Cave as to the definition of the word " banners," and that in this case they were used as marks of distinction, questioned whether a payment for banners not used as marks of distinction would be illegal. Here, however, it was plain that they were used as marks of distinction, and came within the Acts 17 and 18 Vict. chap. 102, and the Act of 1883, combined and construed together.

This, of course, raises a question as to what banners would be illegal, and in what case it would be legitimate to use them. In the course of the argument, Mr. Justice Williams suggested that a very pretty Christmas conundrum would be, " When is a banner not a banner?" It is quite clear that if no *payment* had been made for the banners, and that friends of the respondent had chosen to make them and present them to him, there would have been nothing illegal in so doing; and it is doubtful whether, if these canvases had only had written upon them " Mr. Isaacson's Committee Rooms," as an advertisement of the fact that at that house there was a Committee Room; that could have been said to have been a mark of distinction, and that is probably what was in Mr. Justice Williams' mind when he made the remarks above quoted. It may, however, be considered wiser by those who conduct elections, after this decision of the Court, to refrain from payment for banners of any description.

One other mark of distinction not mentioned in the Corrupt Practices Act came under the consideration of the Judges in the Walsall case, and that was the distribution of a large number of cards with the portrait of the candidate and the words, " Play up, Swifts. James for Walsall." The cards were printed with the portrait of the candidate on the upper part of the card, the lower part of the card having the corners cut off for the purpose of inserting in the hat-band. Although a number of other charges were made against the respondent in this case, the Court based their decision to unseat him on the one point of the payment for the printing of these cards. Mr. Baron Pollock, in the course of his judgment, said, " There was one peculiar case which might affect future elections. He referred to the charge of payment by the election agent for what had been called ' cards.' He was not speaking of the ordering, or distributing, or wearing of hat cards. The charge was that the cards had been worn by a very large number of persons; that the agent for the candidate paid for them, and that the payment was an illegal one, which would set aside the election. He was happy to think that this was not a charge of corrupt practice. It was simply a question whether, and to what extent, the person concerned had been guilty of a breach of the Act. Then the question was—Had he been relieved from it on the ground of inadvertence? The facts amounted in substance to this—that a very large number of the cards were ordered, were supplied, were worn, and were paid for in the account. According to the books of Henry Robinson, 2,000 cards for hats with ' Play up, Swifts' on them were ordered, and 2,000 ditto on stout paper, these being spoken of as cards for hats. Now it was perfectly well known that the election badge used in all elections years ago was beyond all doubt what the statute intended to prohibit. These cards were not merely invitations as of old, but they bore the photographic likeness of the candidate, and words of encouragement to vote for him. So long as cards alone were used there could be no objection, but if such a thing as the present card were made to be placed in the coat; if, as a matter of fact, they were used for that purpose; and then if, after they had been ordered and used for that purpose, and had been so described in the account, the person who paid that account paid it knowing what it was, that was a very different thing from saying, ' I printed the cards and distributed them, but I was not responsible for what was done with them.' The Legislature had decided that they would pro- hibit by penalty any mark of distinction for the obvious reason that it was a party badge. When the recent Act was passed, the Legislature endea-

voured to extinguish mischief of this kind by pre-
venting not only the ordering of such badges, but
the wearing of them."

Probably few elections since the passing of the
Corrupt Practices Act have been held where cards
with the portrait of the candidate have not been
issued : possibly not in the exact form of the one
in question, nor issued for the definite purpose of
being used as a badge, but they have been used on
either side, either to place in the hat, or to pin on
the coat. It will be noted that the Court stated
that so long as cards alone were used there could
be no objection; but if such a thing as the present
card were made to be placed in the hat; if, as a
matter of fact, they were used for that purpose,
and then, if they had been ordered and used for
that purpose, and been so described in the account,
the person who paid that account, paid it knowing
what it was, that was a very different thing from
saying, " I printed the cards and distributed them,
but I was not responsible for what was done with
them."

The above decision, apparently, does not prohibit the printing of cards with the portrait of the
candidate, so long as the letterpress amounts to
nothing more than an invitation to vote for the
candidate.

The Walsall decision was discussed in the East

Clare petition some days later. At that election 3,000 cards were printed and distributed with the words, " Men of Clare, remember Parnell and vote for Redmond," printed upon them, and, it was said, they were worn in the hats of the voters. Mr. Justice O'Brien, in delivering judgment, " was convinced that there was no illegality whatever in the distribution of the cards. The cards, in his opinion, were not party distinctions within the meaning of the Act of Parliament. The Cork card was the usual one soliciting the honour of the vote and interest. From some of the cards the name of the second candidate was erased. The Ennis card says, ' Remember Parnell and vote for Redmond,' which was the same thing, substantially, as to vote for Mr. Redmond, the Parnellite candidate. These were canvassing cards or invitation cards, which in the judgment of the Court in the Walsall case were expressly declared to be innocent. The Walsall case was considered to have gone to the extreme verge of the law. Their lordships in the present case were asked to step across the border into the region of entire and utter absurdity. Anything, no doubt, might be turned into party distinctions, but the party distinctions forbidden must be those that were intended to be used as such, of which there was no evidence in the present case. In the Walsall judgment the object was expressly stated

to be hat cards with the picture of the candidate,
which, at least, Mr. Redmond had spared them in
that case. The cards in the present case were no
such things at all; they had another use altogether,
and the fact that another use was made of them did
not constitute the illegality unless there was specific
evidence from which they might draw the conclusion that the use was illegally intended. There
was no such evidence. Anything, no doubt, might
be made use of as distinctions. It was suggested
by the counsel for the petitioner that a piece of
blank paper or mourning on the hat might be held
to be a mark of distinction. If that argument was
followed into the wider field of feminine ornament,
then the real war would begin as to what was a
distinction."

CHAPTER IV.

It is satisfactory to notice that, among the charges contained in the petitions of 1892, intimidation and undue influence was not included in any of the English or Welsh cases. In Ireland alone such charges not only were made, but were proved by overwhelming evidence, and those who were charged with having exercised intimidation, or who attempted to exercise influence of an illegitimate character, were ministers of religion. It is to be regretted that these gentlemen did not confine themselves to that natural influence which their position gave them.

Both in the North and South Meath elections the clergy seem to have taken a very prominent and active part. The Bishop, Dr. Nulty, issued a pastoral, in which, among other expressions, appear to have been some of the following: "Parnellism saps the very root and strikes at the foundation of Catholic faith"; "No man could remain a Catholic so long as he elects to cling to Parnellism"; "The dying Parnellite himself will hardly dare to face the justice of his Master till he has been prepared

32

and anointed by us for the last awful struggle and
the terrible judgment that will immediately follow
it. I earnestly implore you, then, dearly beloved,
to stamp out by your votes at the coming election
the great moral, social, and religious evil which
has brought about so much disunion and bad blood
amongst a hitherto united people."

The Meath cases justify the action of Parliament in enacting that it shall be illegal to inflict
or threaten to inflict any temporal or spiritual
injury, damage, harm, or loss upon or against any
person in order to induce or compel such person to
vote or refrain from voting.

Evidence was given that priests called voters
who differed with them by objectionable names
likely to arouse the hatred of their fellow towns-
men, and that there were distinct cases of threats
to withhold the sacraments, as well as threats,
which probably appear to be absurd, but yet which
would have great effect upon a peasantry, " to put
fire to their heels and toes," and that if they voted
for the Parnellite candidate they " would go to
hell." Evidence was given that one priest, in
preaching, had described those who canvassed for
the Parnellite candidate as " disreputable indi-
viduals," and " that it would be worse for them
here and hereafter." Of another it was said that
from the altar he stated " that the time had come

when nobody could remain a Catholic and be a
Parnellite," and, striking the altar, he said " that
he knew who would be marked men."

As an instance of the temporal injury which
could be inflicted by one in the position of a priest,
was the case of a pensioner who had been accustomed to have the certificate for his pension signed
by a particular priest. Having been canvassed by
this gentleman, and having refused to vote as
requested, he was informed by the priest, " I will
never sign your papers again." Such a threat to
a man in that position might be expected to have
a very serious influence.

Mr. Justice O'Brien, in the South Meath case,
in delivering judgment, alluded at length to the
evidence of Patrick King, to the effect that he
would be refused the sacraments when dying.
After comparing the words admitted by Father
Tynan with those of the witness King, "it was
impossible not to come to the conclusion that the
language did contain a menace of a certain kind."

Dealing with the priests and the decision of
the question of undue influence, his lordship
observed that "it was laid down in the Longford
case that the clergy had an undoubted right to
take part in elections, and to influence the voters,
but it was not lawful for them to declare it to be a
sin to vote in a different manner from them, or to

threaten to refuse the sacraments. A question of great moment had been introduced into the case, namely, whether the clergy had right to determine what were faith and morals. That was a tremendous authority to claim. It must be observed, however, that the bishop's pastoral did not directly advance such a proposition. He could conceive situations in which the question of moral duty would be involved, but he could not understand how anything affecting the election of a member of Parliament could be held to be a question of moral application, in respect of which it would be a sin to vote in a particular way, and there was no evidence of any theological rule." His lordship then dealt with the pastoral of Dr. Nulty, which was read in the churches on July 30th. It was clear, he said, "that that document had a powerful effect on the community to which it was addressed. It was alleged that the election would strike at the root of the Catholic faith. Although the resolution of the bishops, which was the foundation of that proposition, related solely to the question of political leadership, Dr. Nulty laid it down that no intelligent or well informed person could remain a Roman Catholic and adhere to Parnellism. That would be a startling and tremendous proposition."

" In reference to the remarkable sermons of the Rev. Father O'Connell, who said that he would ' fire the heels and toes' of certain persons, it was admitted by that gentleman himself that he used the words. It was a most extraordinary thing to say. It called back to his mind the scattering of the fire before Vespasian, and the act of that priest was certainly sufficient to scatter a good deal of political incendiarism in his parish."

Reviewing the whole case, his lordship said that, "from a multitude of incidents, it was his opinion that during the election the priests, under a strong idea of obedience to their bishop, did use language calculated to convey to the minds of the voters that their conduct upon this election involved the question of eternal condemnation." Mr. Justice Andrews, in the same case, agreed with Mr. Justice O'Brien's judgment, and remarked : "There were several remarkable cases where clergymen who were agents of the respondent were guilty of undue influence, which amounted to spiritual intimidation." In the North Meath case, in addition to the reading of the pastoral, referred to in the previous case, evidence was given of actual physical violence by the priests. Mr. Justice Andrews, in the course of his judgment, stated : " It had been relied on by the petitioners' counsel that a species of widespread undue spiritual influence had prevailed in the constituency during the election, by which it was maintained harm and loss had been

done to the petitioner in the matter of votes. The
evidence upon this point he had listened to with
deep regret. A number of cases were disclosed of
acts on the part of clergymen which he could not
leave unnoticed. It had been urged on their behalf
that they had unfortunately allowed loss of temper
to betray them into some deplorable acts of personal
violence. In some of the cases women had been
the objects of attack, which could hardly be justi-
fied by any public explanation, and the respondent's
counsel admitted this in addressing the court, and
expressed, on their behalf, regret for what had
occurred. . . . Observations had also been made
to the effect that the clergy must be regarded as
agents of the respondent in relation to such matters
as the promulgation of the bishop's pastoral, and of
the promotion of the effect which it was intended to
produce among the electors. The court entirely
acquitted the respondent of any complicity, direct
or indirect, with acts of personal violence, so gravely
censurable, which had occurred, and the election
could not have been voided thereby ; but about the
bishop's pastoral, in regard to which there was so
much discussion, he had, on a previous occasion,
and after full and careful consideration, arrived at
an opinion which he was unable to change."

He also dealt with the distinction between
spiritual and physical undue influence. The former

383261

was a subtle influence, and in face of the evidence
they had heard of the reading of the pastoral and
of the sermons delivered from the altars by priests
in their vestments, he could not but come to the
conclusion that the effect produced was such in law
as to prevent a free election.

Mr. Justice Johnson, concurring with the judgment of Mr. Justice Andrews, believed that pas-
sages in the pastoral were calculated to exercise
undue influence, and held that the respondent, by
his agents, was clearly responsible for the pastoral.
In both cases the elections were voided.

CHAPTER V.

AGENCY.

ᴵ There is no decided case which lays down in distinct terms what constitutes election agency. Each case has to be dealt with on its merits, and the question has again arisen in some of the recent petitions. A man cannot make himself a sub-agent, nor does the fact that a man wore party colours prove that he was an agent, unless his action has been adopted, or ratified by the candidate in whose interest he has acted. Whether a member of a political association is an agent, for whose illegal acts the candidate is responsible, is entirely a question for an Election Court. In the Worcester case Mr. Baron Pollock held that " a man being a canvasser does not necessarily make him an agent. He might be a most confidential agent, or he might be a man of no standing in the party." In some earlier cases it has been held that an association may be one to whose funds the candidate has contributed, and advocating his cause, and yet for whose acts he is not responsible; while in another case an association supporting his candidature, but not receiving any financial support from him, was found by the judges to be so closely connected with the candidate as to make him responsible for its acts. In

9

the Hexham case, the secretary of a Conservative Association made illegal payments out of funds mainly provided by subscription from the candidate; although not with his knowledge or consent, the candidate was held responsible. (See Hexham, pages 8, 18.)

In the South Meath case the clergy had canvassed for the respondent, and had taken a very active part in the election. Meetings of the clergy had been held, and in many instances they had been appointed by the respondent as personation agents. Mr. Justice O'Brien's remark upon this was: "It was difficult to say if they were not the principals, and Mr. Fulham (the candidate) merely an agent." Mr. Justice Andrews, in the same case, said: "The motive power in the election of Mr. Fulham was the clergy, of whom he had availed himself, and to whom he acknowledged thanks when he was elected. Mr. Fulham made the priests his agents, and their action voided the election under the section of the Act of 1883 referring to undue influence."

At Rochester the Conservative party had organised a club known as the Rochester Constitutional Birthnight Club. The respondent was a member of the club and subscribed to its funds. The chairman of the club, on the occasion of his own birthday, treated the members of the club, which met at the Conservative club, to refreshments. The respondent was present at the gathering and responded to the toast of his health. The Court held that the chairman was an agent of the respondent.

In the Montgomery case, where an habitual drinker had been elected on to the respondent's committee, it was admitted that he treated indiscriminately, but he stated to the Court that he had not canvassed for the respondent. Mr. Baron Pollock seemed to consider that it was very unlikely "that people should have selected an agent of that kind, with the intention that he should go about bribing, by the very reason of his frailty. People who selected a man of that kind must have a perfect knowledge that the instrument they had chosen would probably afford the strongest evidence against themselves," and he accordingly exonerated him from any corrupt motive. This extraordinary dictum followed remarks from the same Judge that there were doubtless people who were unaware that he was a man given to habits of intemperance; "but there were many others, probably the majority, who did know his habits, and who looked upon him with feelings of commiseration for his position, and also as a man useful to the people who employed him."

Justice Wills, however, dissented from this view of the case. (See page 21.)

CHAPTER VI.

The question when election expenses begin is one which must be determined by the circumstances of each particular case. The words of the Act— section 8, " before, during, and after an election " —are very wide, and the only cases before the Courts in 1892 in which the question arose were at Rochester and Stepney. At Rochester a conversazione was organised by the local Conservative Association, and the Judges decided that, looking at the time at which it was held, and that it was the obvious intention of those who took part in it to promote the return of the respondent; if the entertainment had been innocent throughout, nevertheless, it must necessarily have been returned as portion of the election expenses of the candidate. Mr. Justice Cave said: " It was impossible to say that only those expenses were to be returned which were incurred after the writ was issued. The time which elapsed in many cases between the issue of the writ and the date of the election was too short to admit of the necessary preparations being made of conducting the election, and it was absolutely essential that preparations of that kind should be begun and expenses be incurred in anticipation of the issue of the writ. There was nothing in the Act which forbade expenses being incurred before the issue of the writ; there was nothing in the Act which forbade the candidate to incur such expenses. The Act, no doubt, required that they should be paid by the election agent, and so long as they were paid by the election agent it did not require that they should in all cases be incurred by him."

In the Stepney case, evidence was given of the holding of two meetings by the association, at which resolutions were passed in support of the candidature of the respondent, before the appointment of the election agent. The Court held that such meetings should have been included in the election expenses (see page 14). In the same case the Court pointed out the danger of work done for registration becoming confused with work done for an election, and thus the provisions of the Act as to the limitation of election expenses being evaded. Mr. Justice Cave said: "It is a dangerous course, therefore, unless the election agent can make it quite clear that he has not been doing election work under the guise of registration work, and if not, he must not be surprised if election judges suspect that he has been muddling the accounts together in order to escape from the fetters of the Act of Parliament."

CHAPTER VII.

Although the rule is that seven days before the trial the petitioner should give particulars of the charges relied on, it is within the discretion of the Court to extend that time, and this was done in the Stepney case, when the Court ordered that they should be delivered ten days before the day fixed for the hearing. Mr. Baron Pollock said : "The cases showed that it was in the discretion of the Court to require a longer time for notice of the charges than seven days; and in this case, considering the number of the electors and of the charges likely to be made, ten days did not appear an unreasonable time."

In the Manchester case, it was alleged that " the respondent was, by his agents, guilty of illegal practices by hiring, for the purpose of the conveyance of electors to and from the poll at the said election, carriages and horses, knowing that the owners thereof were prohibited, by section 14 of the Corrupt and Illegal Practices Prevention Act, 1883, from lending the same for that purpose." It was contended that the offence complained of

44

would have to be proved to have been done by the candidate, or by his election agent, and that no such allegation having been made, the particulars must fail. The Court declined to amend, and struck out that portion of the particulars. Further, on the question of general treating in the same case, where it was alleged that a particular event had taken place " before, during, and after " the 6th July, and it was endeavoured to be proved that the event had taken place on a particular day, the Court held that such a mode of giving a date was perfectly inadmissible. It would have been just as as well to have left the date column blank.

In the Central Finsbury Election Petition the question was raised whether the respondent was entitled to go into cases contained in the petitioner's particulars, but which the petitioner himself withdrew. It was argued, on behalf of the petitioner, that the list before the Court referred to the joint lists of the petitioner and the respondent. The Court held that the respondent was not entitled to object to votes not in the list which he had prepared, and Mr. Justice Cave, in giving judgment, said : " The rule required the name to be in ' the list,' which meant the objector's list. The petitioner would not come prepared to defend the votes in his own list of objections. The proper construction of the rule was that either party must put into his own list of objections the names of voters he proposed to attack."

Application was then made for leave to amend the respondent's particulars by inserting the name which he wished to object to, but which was on the petitioner's list. The Court decided that that could not be done, as a matter of course, and that it could only be applied for on affidavit, stating sufficient grounds for the application.

In the same case a question arose as to the right of the Court to ask a voter for whom he had had voted before his ballot paper had been identified, the difficulty having arisen through two ballot papers being found marked with the same number. The Court solved the difficulty by placing both ballot papers before the voter; he, having chosen one as the one he had marked, the Court proceeded to hear the evidence against his right to vote.

CHAPTER VIII.

It was objected in the Central Finsbury case
that two persons who were employed as bill posters
were, by reason of their employment, disqualified
from voting. It was proved that the bill posting
was done in the ordinary course of their business;
that, although some portion of it was done by themselves, the greater portion was done by their
employés. It was argued that under Section 25 of
the Ballot Act this was an employment of a
"voter" at the election. Mr. Justice Williams put
the case of a printer employed to print the posters,
and said the line must be drawn somewhere, and
that would clearly be outside the enactment.

It was also alleged that the bill poster had
employed "sandwichmen," and that that was an
illegal employment. Mr. Justice Cave characterised
this argument as "monstrous," and said the votes
were clearly good. The voter in such case was not
employed to do the work himself, any more than
the printer of a newspaper who inserts advertisements.

It was likewise objected that a person who
received two sums of 8s. and 2s. for cleaning a

47

schoolroom in which meetings were held, was a
person who had been employed for payment by the
respondent. It was proved that the voter's wife
was the caretaker of the schools, that the voter
assisted her in that position, that he arranged the
room for two meetings for both sides, and was paid
for his services for preparing the platform, etc.
The Court held that it did not come within the
Act.

CHAPTER IX.

Where a person's name is entered in more than one division of a borough, and neither of those qualifications is his place of abode, and no mark is placed against either entry to show that he is not entitled to vote for that qualification, and if under those circumstances he should vote in both divisions, the question will arise as to which vote was given first. The one given first will be valid, and the other, on a scrutiny, struck out. But where a voter is on the register for two divisions, and one of those entries is for his place of abode, he is not entitled to vote otherwise than for his place of abode. The Registration Act, 48 Vic., cap. 15, sec. 5, sub-sec. 2, provides : " Where a Parliamentary Borough is divided into divisions, and, notwithstanding the said provisions of the Parliamentary and Municipal Registration Act, 1878, and this Act, the name of a person is entered in the Register of Parliamentary Voters in more than one division in the said Parliamentary Borough without such note as above in this section mentioned, and one of those entries is his place of abode, he shall be entitled to vote only in that division in which he is registered as a voter in respect of his place of

E 4

abode, and shall not vote in respect of any other entry." In the case in question before the Court, in the Central Finsbury petition, the voter had voted in both divisions and was on the register in each division described as occupying a dwelling-house, whereas in one case it should have been described as "shop" or "tenement."

The Court decided that the voter had voted wrongly. Mr. Justice Cave said: "The Registration Act had a provision that where a voter had two qualifications in a borough the barrister was to mark where the voter was to vote, and if not, then the voter was only to vote in the division where his place of abode was. In this case the voter was entered in two divisions, and should have voted for the division in which his place of abode was—that is the Holborn division. It was true that in both divisions the house was described as 'dwelling-house,' but he was registered 'in respect of his place of abode' in the Holborn division, and he could not be registered in the Central division 'in respect of his place of abode.' If he had been registered for a shop, yet if he resided there he would be registered 'in respect of his place of abode,' but here he was only registered in respect of his place of abode in the Holborn division, and there he should have voted. The vote was therefore bad."

CHAPTER X.

DISPUTED BALLOT PAPERS.

Under Rule 36, Ballot Act, 1872, the Returning Officer is to reject ballot papers when they come under the several heads of either (1) Want of official mark, (2) Voting for more candidates than entitled to, (3) Writing or mark by which the voter could be identified, or (4) Unmarked or void for uncertainty.

In the Cirencester petition, papers were rejected by the Returning Officer under the first, third, and fourth heads. The Returning Officer provided rubber stamps to stamp with ink the official mark.

WANT OF OFFICIAL MARK.

The Court (Hawkins and Vaughan Williams, JJ.) decided that the official mark must have been actually impressed upon the ballot paper by the Presiding Officer; and where the ballot paper only showed a mark which had evidently come off another paper, and had not been stamped on by the Presiding Officer, the Court held it to be void. Where the ballot paper had no official mark on the back, the Court held the votes bad; but where the ballot paper was stamped on the front, and the ink had run through so as to be seen on the back, although the stamp had not been applied to the

51

back, the Court held it sufficient. Where the official mark on the back was imperfect and indistinctly stamped, it was held to satisfy the section. This applied to faint impressions on some of the ballot papers.

MARK BY WHICH VOTER COULD BE IDENTIFIED.

Under the third head, the Court held that any mark by which the voter *can* be identified invalidated the vote, but not any by which he *might* be identified.

VOID FOR UNCERTAINTY.

Under the fourth head, the Court held that where no mark appeared on face of ballot paper, but a cross was marked in pencil on the back of the paper, it was void. They held, however, that wherever there was a mark on the front of the paper which indicated the intention of the voter it would be counted, although the mark was an imperfect one. Some of the papers were unmarked by pen or pencil, but there appeared an indented mark as if made by a thumb nail. The Court reserved judgment on these cases, along with others; but, in giving their decision on the reserved cases, declined to give reasons for the decision in individual cases, and, therefore, it is only to be inferred from the decision above referred to that they were counted as good. The Court concluded to declare an equality of votes, and voided the election.

The following votes were held to be good for Lawson :—*

4917

1	LAWSON	⚹
2	MASTER	

11761

1	LAWSON	✕
2	MASTER	

4591

1	LAWSON	✕
2	MASTER	

The following were held to be good for
Master :—

8633

1	LAWSON	
2	MASTER ✗	

3452

1	LAWSON	
2	MASTER	✗

5702

1	LAWSON	●
2	MASTER	✗

By Sec. 13 of the Ballot Act, 1872, it is enacted that "no election shall be declared invalid by reason of a non-compliance with the rules contained in the first schedule to this Act, or any mistake in the use of the forms in the second schedule to this Act, if it appears to the tribunal having cognizance of the question that the election was conducted in accordance with the principles laid down in the body of this Act, and that such non-compliance or mistake did not affect the *result* of the election."

In the East Clare petition it was proved that in one polling booth the Presiding Officer, in ignorance, handed the voters both the ballot paper and the counterfoil attached. About 190 of these were marked by voters, and put in that condition into the ballot box.

In the case of Woodward *v.* Sarson, L.R. 10 CP., the Court held 294 ballot papers invalid, where the Presiding Officer had marked upon the face of the paper the register number of the voter, by means of which the voter could have been identified. They held, however, that as the decision did not affect the *result* of the election, the election was not void. In a later case, Thornbury, 2 *Times* L.R. 485-490, it was held that to render the vote bad, the mark which identified the voter must have been made by himself, and that the act of a Presiding

Officer in wrongly marking a paper would not invalidate the vote.

In the East Clare case, 1892, however, the Court followed the decision in Woodward *v.* Sarson; but held that a non-compliance with the rules did not void the election, unless the result of the election was affected by it.

CHAPTER XI.

The power of the Election Court to grant relief is regulated by sec. 23 of the Corrupt and Illegal Practices Act, 1883. That section provides that where any act or omission by the candidate or agent would be, but for that section, an illegal practice, payment, employment, or hiring, the Court, if they see fit, may except the candidate or agent from the consequences of such act or omission.

The Court must, however, come to the conclusion that such act or omission arose from inadvertence or from accidental miscalculation, or from some other reasonable cause of a like nature, and that it did not arise from any want of good faith. Notice of the application must be given in the county or borough where the election occurred before the application for relief is made, and must be given a sufficient time before the application is made. What is a sufficient time is a question for the Court. This power of relieving a candidate and his agent was exercised in several of the petitions in 1892, but in no case so remarkably as in the Stepney petition.

In that case the agent admitted in his evidence that he had destroyed all his memoranda and a book in which he had kept note of his expenditure. That these were destroyed after notice of the petition. He admitted one payment for services to a voter who voted. It was proved that he had ordered and paid for banners through a third party, that he had omitted the payment from his election return, and he admitted that he did so because he thought the payment illegal. It was also proved that a number of omissions had been made in the election return of moneys expended by him in the election.

No application for relief was made until the fourth day of the hearing, after all these matters had been proved, when application was made to relieve the respondent for thirty-six illegal acts either of omission or commission.

The Court (Mr. Justice Cave and Mr. Justice Vaughan Williams) animadverted strongly on the destruction of the book and memoranda, held that the banners were illegal, but, notwithstanding, held there was no want of *bonâ fides*, and granted relief.

That this was a stretching of the powers of the Court no one acquainted with the Act can doubt. In the Walsall case, Mr. Baron Pollock intimated, when counsel suggested that the respondent should apply for relief, that "that provision was only intended for the assistance of persons who were innocent."

In the Rochester case, Mr. Justice Williams, on an application to grant relief, pointed out that there was only one corrupt practice with which they could connect the respondent, and that " if this were the only matter with which they had to deal, he should himself feel that this was an occasion in which they ought to exercise the powers which had been bestowed upon them by section 22 of the Corrupt and Illegal Practices Act, 1883. (Mr. Justice Cave, " Hear, hear ; I quite agree.") He thought the intention of this Act of Parliament was to draw the strings of the law as tightly round corrupt and illegal practices at elections as they possibly could be, but at the same time he thought the law intended by sections 22 and 23 to enable judges to relieve candidates from all responsibility for corrupt and illegal practices where they had satisfied the judges that they had done everything on their part to render the election pure and free from corruption." (Note the decision by the same judges in the Stepney case, *ante*, p. 58.)

CHAPTER XII.

The costs of an election petition are absolutely in the discretion of the Election Court, and they have the power to direct on what scale the costs shall be allowed and taxed. Although usually costs follow the event, the Court may deprive the petitioner of costs, although allegations in the petition have been proved which render the seat voidable, or they may deprive the respondent of costs when the petition fails.

It remained, however, for the Court in the Stepney case to decide, not only to give costs to the respondent on such particulars as the petitioners either withdrew or failed to prove, but also to grant him half costs out of the £1,000 deposited in Court by the petitioners on those charges in the petition which had been proved against the respondent, and for which the Court thought fit to grant relief.

The petitioners in the case were both working men; one, however, was a County Councillor for the division on the London County Council. They admitted that they were not possessed of means to pay costs, and that the deposit of £1,000 had been found for them.

This surprising decision is a very serious one, and practically strikes at the possibility of petitioning, unless the petitioners are either wealthy persons or give some security or make some arrangements to pay their opponents' costs beyond the £1,000 deposit. In a working-class constituency such as Stepney, this may mean the deprivation of the electorate of the power to question the illegal acts of a rich candidate. The petitioners must be persons who have a direct interest in the election, and it may be impossible to find one or more persons who are aggrieved by the result of the election, who are able to command the necessary funds beyond the deposit.

The question of "maintenance" was raised by counsel for the respondent on the ground that the deposit had been found by persons outside the constituency, but the Court decided that that was a question which they, as election judges, could not entertain. They intimated that the question could only be raised by a substantive motion in the Queen's Bench Division.

In the Walsall case petitioners were granted costs on all the points where they had either succeeded or the other side had asked for relief. The other costs were directed to follow the event.

In the Hexham, East Clare, Worcester, and North Meath cases costs followed the judgment.

In the South Meath case costs were given to the petitioners who succeeded, except on the charges of bribery and treating, of which the Court held there was no evidence, and costs on these points were given to the respondent against the petitioner.

In the Rochester case the Court gave the petitioners general costs, the respondent being unseated. With reference to charges of bribery, which the Court held had failed, if they had caused any extra expenditure to respondent, petitioners were ordered to pay them; and on the charges of treating, the Court being of opinion that the respondent was personally innocent, no costs were allowed on either side.

In the Montgomery case, where the judges differed in their judgment, and the petition was dismissed in consequence, the respondent was allowed his costs, except on the points upon which the judges disagreed, and in those cases each party were ordered to pay their own costs.

The Central Finsbury petition was withdrawn, by consent of the Court, on the terms of each party paying their own costs.

In the Cirencester case, the Court deciding that there was an equality of votes, ordered each party to pay their own costs.

INDEX.

ABODE. place of, voting for, 50.
Agency, 12, 40, 41.
Associations, entertainment by,
9, 10, 13, 19; agency of,
41; when action by, legi-
timate, 10, 13, 14; not necessarily agents, 10; need
not cease work because of
elections, 11; subscription
of candidate to, 13; sus-
pension of work during
elections, 13; meetings
convened by, 14; Licensed
Victuallers', 16.

Badges, 28.
Ballot Paper, identification of,
52; want of official mark,
51; identification of voter,
53; specimens of marked,
53; with counterfoil at-
tached, 55.
Banners, 24–26.
Bands, 23.
Bill posters, 47.
Birthnight Clubs, 19, 40.
Bishop's Pastoral, 32.
Brewers' Association, expendi-
ture by, 15.

Candidate, when responsible
for acts of Association,
10; subscription to Asso-
ciation, 13, 14.
Cards, portrait, 27.
Caretaker of schools, payment
to, 48.
Committee-man, treating by, 21.
Concerts, smoking, 11.

Conversazioni, 11, 42.
Costs, 60.

Deficiency in cost of entertainment, payment for, 9. 18.
Divisions, voting in two, 49.
Dwelling-house: voter to vote
for place of abode, 50.

Election expenses: meetings
held by Associations, 14,
42; Licensed Victuallers,
not to be included, 16.
Election expenses before issue
of writ, 43.
Employment of voter, 47.
Entertainments, 8, 9, 11, 18. 42.
Executive Committee may be
agents, 10–14.

Hat cards, 27, 30.

Identification of voter by mark
on ballot paper, 52.
Illegal payments from Association funds, 10, 18, 49.

Licensed Victuallers' Association, expenditure by, 15.

Mark, official, on ballot paper,
51.
Marking ballot paper, 52.
Marks of distinction, 23, 27.
Meetings convened by Associa-
tion before election, 12, 14,
43; Licensed Victuallers'
Association, 15.

Official mark on ballot paper, 51.

Particulars, time for giving 44; sufficiency of, 44; right of petitioner to go into case of respondent, 45.
Picnics, 11.
Priests, undue influence by, 32; agency of, 40.
Primrose League, 10.

Railway fares at reduced price, 10.
Refreshments, 9.
Registration, 10, 43.
Relief, when granted, 57, 59.

Sandwichmen, 47.

Smoking concerts, 11, 19.
Spiritual injury, threat of, 33, 37.
Subscription to Association by candidate, 11, 14.

Temporal injury, 34.
Trade associations, 15.
Treating, 9, 11, 18, 19; by publicans, 20; habitual, 21, 41.

Undue influence, 32.

Voting in more than one division, 49.
Voter's name, unstarred, 49.

HAYMAN CHRISTY & LILLY, LTD. PRINTERS 113 FARRINGDON RD. E C.

UNIVERSITY OF CALIFORNIA

www.ingramcontent.com/pod-product-compliance
Lightning Source LLC
Chambersburg PA
CBHW021630270326
41931CB00008B/953